D1570639

Snappy Sassy Salty
Wise Words for Authors and Writers

Inside this gem of a book, Judith Briles delivers wise words for the author's soul … you'll want to keep it as a reference and read it over and over.
>   —Dan Poynter, The Book Futurist

Judith is one of the best voices in the industry. She's a driver, a polished professional and really knows her stuff. If you want solid advice and some serious motivation, you'll love this book!
>   —Penny C. Sansevieri
>   CEO Author Marketing Experts, Inc.
>   and Adjunct Professor, NYU

Judith Briles is one smart (and sassy) lady. She's one of the people I rely on over and over for the wisest advice on publishing books. This book shares some of her wisest and saltiest advice.
>   —John Kremer, author of *1001 Ways to Market Your Books* and blogger at *BookMarketingBestsellers.com*

Straight and to the point! This book contains the information EVERY author requires to be successful in a highly competitive industry. If you are looking for success, look no further than the "wise words" from Judith Briles. She's the master.

—Peggy McColl
New York Times best-selling author

It's pretty rare that you learn what you need to know while having a rip-roaring time of it. Writers, both seasoned and novice alike, will be thanking Judith Briles for years to come for her newest offering: *Snappy, Sassy, Salty*. This is the real deal, the stuff you need to know that you didn't even know you needed to know. Judith does what she does best: help authors and writers launch! This latest offering is the best yet, incredibly informative, fresh, fun, uber creative, and of course, snappy, sassy and salty!

—Tammy Bleck
Author, speaker, blogger extraordinaire of
WittyWomanWriting.com/blog

At last … the perfect "little book" for we authors and writers. It's fun. It's insightful. It works.

—Rick Frishman
Publisher and best-selling author

Judith Briles delivers the full range of publishing experience, from the big NY houses to the rapidly-accelerating independent zone. Most importantly, she's dominated in both worlds. Nobody in the business is a better teacher and shepherd.

—Dom Testa
Author, speaker, radio host

Judith is THE Master Book Shepherd. My award-winning book would have never been completed without her Snappy, Sassy and Salty words of wisdom. Judith's newest book is truly a gift to the book world!

—Lynn Hellerstein, author of
See It. Say It. Do It!

Whether you need inspiration, insight, encouragement, straight-talk—or a swift kick in the pants—it's all here in this brief little book by Briles. Love it!

—Dianna Booher, Author of
Creating Personal Presence
and *Communicate With Confidence*

Dr. Judith Briles has a wealth of knowledge and experience as a book publisher, author, and problem solver and I am honored to be a colleague and friend.

—Dave Raymond
Thomson-Shore, Inc., West Sales Manager

Judith Briles is not The Book Shepherd she calls herself. She is an author's North Star, guiding light, and a rock star for all of us with a hunger to write.

—Bob Vanourek
co-author of Triple Crown Leadership

Juice up your writing. A must for all sassy writers. Briles has done it again!"

—Anne Randolph
Stories Gathered at the Kitchen Table

Judith Briles has done it again. She's written yet another "must have" book for authors and done so in a witty yet highly informative fashion.

I was intrigued with the title, sweet and salty (gotta love that combination—yum!) and the content continued to please.

If you are a writer who aspires to be an author, or already are an author whose stuck on your current book and need some inspiration and direction to make it happen, Judith's bite size pieces of advice will do just that. My personal favorite?

Smart authors become savvy positioners. They do it with Clarity, Confidence, Competence and Commitment,
as quoted by none other than, Judith Briles!

—Susan Gilbert, Best-selling author and CEO of Online Promotion Success, Inc.

There are hundreds of variables that go into the making and marketing of a successful book. Judith's book brings them all together in a logical, yet sassy way that will take you and your book to the next level.

—Brian Jud, Executive Director of APSS
and author of *How to Make
Real Money Selling Books*

It is simply amazing to see author's careers, and even lives, be transformed by the guiding light called Judith Briles. Her experience and expertise in authoring, publishing and marketing are in full sassy swing in this snappy little gem.

I've no doubt if Lewis & Clark needed a Book Shepherd during their explorations, Judith Briles would be leading the pack.

—Nick Zelinger, author and
award-winning book designer

Snappy
Sassy
Salty

Author U Founder
Judith Briles

Snappy

Sassy

Salty

Wise Words for Authors and Writers

Mile High Press, Ltd.
www.MileHighPress.com
MileHighPress@aol.com
303-627-9179

© 2014 Judith Briles

Although every precaution has been taken to verify the accu-
racy of the information contained herein, the author and publisher assume no responsibility for any errors or omissions.
No liability is assumed for damages that may result from the
use of information contained within.

Books may be purchased in quantity
by contacting the publisher directly:
Mile High Press, Ltd., PO Box 460880
Aurora, CO, 80046 or by calling 303-627-9179

Editing: John Maling, EditingByJohn@aol.com
Cover and Interior Design: Nick Zelinger, NZGraphics.com
Illustrations: Don Sidle, www.DonSidle.com

Briles, Judith,
    Snappy, Sassy, Salty: Wise Words for Authors and Writers

ISBN: 978-1-885331-49-6 (hard cover)
ISBN: 978-1-885331-50-2 (e-book)
LCCN: 2013949897

1. Publishing   2. Self-Publishing   3. Author   4. Writer

First Edition   Printed in the United States

Contents

Welcome to My World...

... a world I never imagined that I would be in. The only hint that my ultimate vocation would become writing and speaking about, first emerged in third grade. I got in trouble. In fact, I was in trouble a lot. You see, I talked too much. And I passed notes to my friends in the classroom. Teachers didn't like that. I thought it was normal.

It wasn't until decades later when I was the President of a college foundation in Northern California, that, real writing became a gleam in my eye. A book. Of course, it was to be just one book. But it didn't start out as a book idea; it started out as a dinner.

As the president of the foundation, there were perks—one was that I was always included in the private dinner held for our guest lecturers. Our speaker was my dinner companion one evening. We had a lovely time; laughing and commiserating about

1

each having teenagers. Little did I know that he was actively listening, chalking up a slew of ideas that he would turn into a column based on things I said during the three hours we were together.

A week later when I was on a business trip, I discovered his column in the *Los Angeles Times* with all my ideas around raising teenagers. Oh, the column was amusing, but I wasn't feeling so amused. In fact, I was a tad ticked—he never asked permission or even told me he was thinking about writing about our conversation. Upon my return, there was a letter thanking me for the evening and telling me (warning me?) that he might use some of my ideas in a future column. It was signed, *Cheers— Art Buchwald.*

Future? How about past tense?

Yet, the "aha" dropped in—my epiphany. All that ran through my mind was, "If I don't start taking some of my own ideas, others will take them … and make money." That was April of 1979. By December, I had sold my first book.

Writing too many notes in school, and getting caught. Talking too much and actually being sent home multiple times because I couldn't keep still or quiet. I didn't and wouldn't follow all the rules. Who would have known that they were precursors to my livelihood: being an author and being a professional speaker.

Whatever, whoever, why-ever you are driven to being an author and writer, celebrate it. Go with the flow; know that you will hit plenty of hazards in your journey. It's normal.

Over the years, I've created quotes, the ones for authoring and publishing are included within these pages. One of my personal favorites and one that I tell all my author clients to write down is: *Don't do well what you have no business doing.*

3

When writing, it's your world. Don't let others take your sage advice, storylines and ideas. Stay focused and just go for it. What "it" turns out to be may literally morph your world.

Judith

Author
and Writer Juice:

A Daily Glass
Is All You Need

Wouldn't you love to be able to pick up a pen/pencil or open a blank document on your computer and breeze through the article or chapter you are thinking about ... basically having it completed within a short period of time? Or how about structuring the marketing program you've been thinking about for the past six months, but somehow summer got in the way? Your desk is clear—calendar open and there are no hiccups or obstacles to block your creative waves ... yet ... yet, it's just not flowing. You need some Juice.

You just may have Author or Writer Fatigue Syndrome! The brain cells have taken a hiatus. You are pooped and a cruise is sounding mighty fine right now! If you are feeling a tad overwhelmed ... or just plain blocked on going forward, try these tips to get you back on track:

7

1. Take a piece of paper and divide it into four sections.

In the upper left, label it *ASAP*—those are the items you need, *really* need to deal with. In the upper right, put *7 Days*—these items you have to address within the next seven days—the order of importance is not relevant. In the lower left, write *30 Days*— these are the items/events you need to tackle within the next month. The last column should be labeled *Future*. There's no rush in dealing with any items in that list.

Now, go back to the first *ASAP* section— items that need your immediate attention. One option is to cross one or several off the list with a decision that they can't be dealt with and are in the wrong box. Items in the *30 Days* box are to be ignored for now, as are those in the *Future* and *7 Days* boxes. You are dealing with *ASAP*. Stay focused—it's so much easier to acknowledge that you can't deal/do something in the here and now but can address it next week … then let next week arrive. Meanwhile, the *ASAP* list gets whittled down.

2. Review what you've already created/done.

Sometimes just a review will create the goose that can lay your golden egg. That idea that got buried may be stimulated; the scribbly notes you made all of a sudden make sense; or the original idea you had may take on a whole new dimension because you've let it sit in a form of stew for a while.

3. It's gaze in the belly button time.

What's up? Any thoughts on why you've been stuck or chosen not to go forward with your article, book, work … what? Acknowledge issues preventing you from moving forward. Maybe you don't love the topic or subject any longer. Maybe there's been breaking news or a morphing in the field that has altered your views. Maybe the hero of your story is really a dud. No matter what, look in the mirror and have a chat with yourself. One of my favorite Keepers is—*Don't do well what you have no business doing.* If your work involves pulling teeth … your own … stop it. It's not fun any longer.

4. Review your goals and game plan. Did you ever have any?

That's part of the gaze in the belly button time. Good idea to start here. Goal setting can get you back in the frame of mind that you initially had when you started your authoring venture. If you didn't do it, stop and do it now. I can get blue in the face, reminding you that you've got to have the Vision for what you are doing coupled with the Passion for the project and the Commitment to see it through. When you do run into a hiccup, you've set up the game plan that got you started in the first place. Then it's much easier to cross over the hurdles that pop up.

5. Plan a reward for yourself.

I'm the first to admit—I've been known to start here. Okay ... if I finish this chapter, I get an entire bag of M & Ms—a big one ... and I've done that (you've heard of "baby fat"? This is "book fat"! If I finish this book ... I get an entire month off of reading any business books and I get to read trashy novels—murder mysteries for 30 days in a row. Hot spit!

- When I finish this, I'm booking a cruise to a warm place ...

- When the first draft is done, I'm going skiing ...

- When this section is sent to the editor, I'm watching all the Oscar® winners.

- When I complete this article, I'm ...

You get the picture. Rewards work. So do incentives. Everyone has different ones that they march to. Find yours. Write them down. And honor them. Just having something you want—even a trivial Snickers (only one!) or a night of watching reruns of *The Good Wife* qualifies—it may just be the perk you need to get you back on track or celebrate a job well-done.

6. Escape to the familiar or unfamiliar … just escape.

I don't have the gift of the novelist. Oh, I've worked with authors who wear the fiction hat—tweaking their words and getting the storylines to flow. I've even had to step in, doing massive re-writes, ghosting a great deal of the book—but the initial idea was generated from the author.

I dearly love a great story; yet I don't have the gift of the creative gene that seeds the fiction writer's journey—that sometimes wild-ass idea that delivers magic to the eyes of the reader. What I do know is that when I'm stuck and I pick up something else, leaving my "get this finished" work alone for a day or two, it's amazing how my own creative juices can salivate with ideas that get kick-started with something totally unrelated. Kind of like taking a shower and all of a sudden the "aha" dropping in as the hot water pounds on your shoulders and your stuckiness goes down the drain.

The something else can be fiction … it can be non-fiction … it can be related to your specific genre. The trick is to let another voice come in … think of it as a muse swirling around you … waiting to be invited into your mind and expressed through your fingertips.

7. Know what your writing environment is.

I'm always amused when I listen to an interview with an author who proclaims that getting up at four every morning and writing for four straight hours is the way to be a successful author. Really? It sure isn't mine. Not that I'm averse to getting up at 4 a.m. if that's what the body is saying to do … what I rebel against is someone else telling me how I should write—the time frames, the place, the anything. Coffee bars aren't my thing either—although I have many clients who thrive in that atmosphere—and I encourage them to go there ... often.

I'm a binge writer—have always been; most likely, will always be. I spend days, weeks, even months discussing it in my head; gathering tidbits of info that I've dropped into a "just in case" file or an expandable file that is actually split up in chapters that will be in the "book."

When I move into my writing mode—it's fast, furious and usually on target. I can bang out a first draft of a book in a

short period of time. Recently, I taped the
entire audio program … from scratch … in
two days for the new audio and workbook
series to accompany *Author YOU: Creating
and Building Your Author and Book Platforms.*
Granted, my butt was a tad sore because
I was on the rug in my office, with papers
spread around, mic in hand, voice ready.
When completed, the tapes were overnighted
to the editor. I headed for a cruise four
days later.

No one … and I mean no one … is/was
allowed in my private office space when
I move into that frame—it's as if there is
a yellow crime scene tape across the French
doors to my space. Music is on in the
background … my "reward" is close by
and the fingers are ready. When I come
out to take a health break, get a cup of tea,
I check in with staff if my input is needed
anywhere—otherwise, I'm viewed as "out
of sight, out of mind" to all.

Authors and writers have habits … find the ones that work for you, not someone else. Tell those who come into your space your "rules," your "habits"— and that includes the kids. Too many times, when you are at work, you may be the only one that understands that—you are at work. Education is in order. The Author and Writer Fatigue Syndrome are in the shadows.

The journey to and through authordom is long and loaded with detours and hiccups. And that's just creating the book or your article. The journey that you will go on to support the book has even more.

Take care of yourself. Take care of your book. Reach for the Juice. And do think about that cruise!

If there is a 50-50 chance
something will go wrong,
it will.

Don't think like
everyone else; read
something different.

Don't put off reading
the books you really
want to read. You may
not get the chance.

Problems make the world
go round ... *nonfiction
writers solve them.*

There is a distinction
between authors and
writers. All authors are
writers, but not all
writers are authors.

If the reader for the book
is not ALIVE in the author's
mind, it's yesterday's poop.

Commitment means
time, energy and *money*.
Nothing more, nothing
less. Without it, your
vision and writing
go nowhere.

When it comes to creating
your book, *don't do well
what you have no
business doing.*

If you never say NO,
your "yeses" are worthless.

Keep on learning as you write … your brain loves and thrives on change. When in thrival mode, **new ideas and creativity flow**.

Keep away from people who stomp on your *Vision* for you and your book. Little people always do that—they are envious. *Ahhh*, but the great ones are your cheerleaders— they instill in you that you, too, can soar.

When creating your book, be myopic with whom you let into your space. They must be supporters and encouragers. All others are energy suckers. Delete.

You and your book are only as good as those you hire to bring your vision and words alive.

Be an awesome author! *Break rules. Challenge.* Entertain. Be outrageous. Solve problems. *Deliver answers.*

*Authoring and Writing are
like being in a kaleidoscope.
Sometimes you feel fractured
and broken; other times,
you are swept into a labyrinth
of color and wonder.*

Rarely is there an only
book for an author.

Smart authors and
writers recognize that
they are *entrepreneurs*.

We have an addiction in our house. It's called books.

Welcome All Book Addicts.

Don't be so clever with your words that others are clueless as to what you said.

Words to run from:
*"Hello—I'm from Author
House and I'm here to help
you with your book."*

Publishing predators
suck and *drain* the heart
and soul of the author.

Never work with anyone or a
company that you haven't done
a Google search with the word
*complaint, scam, con, ripoff,
problems, publishing predator*
or *lawsuit* after it. Read
everything. You are warned.

BEWARE of Publishing Predators ... they promise the author-to-be publishing *heaven* and deliver them publishing *hell*.

Books remain unfinished too often. It's one for the money, two for the show, three to get ready, three to get ready, three to get ready ... *break out and go*.

Perfection is usually the enemy of the author. *Finish it. Publish it.* Revised and second editions are always possible.

There isn't an author who wouldn't do a *tweak* here and there on his or her published book.

*A*ll books need a "cold edit"—the final read post layout before printing.

If your book looks like it's been self-published, *don't publish it.*

26

With the publishing
of your first word,
vulnerability steps in.
With your first book,
you are stark naked.

*Do you share your words ...
or do you choose to keep
them invisible?*
Get published.

Your book cover is
the beacon to the reader,
the lighthouse to your
words. Does it say come
to me? Or does it say,
ho-hum, look
somewhere else?

Literary Tragedy:
when words mean
something and they
never get published.

Author Beware:
Publishing Predators
will love you until your
credit card maxes out.

Caution: Author at work.
Do not cross.

When your book is published,
authors become vulnerable.
The critics start poking
and preying, secretly envious
that they didn't have the
vision or the guts to put
their words on display.

Caution:
Author at work.
Keep away and out ...
and out of the way.

Let your fingers
do your talking and
get out of their way.

Sometimes a great sentence contains just a single
word.

Women of the night have more integrity than most publishers: they tell you what you are going to get; how much it will cost; and how long it will take.

Know who you are as an author. Your dog's admiration is secondary.

It's humbling to say it's impossible or can't be done and watch someone else do it flawlessly.

*Y*ou will always have skeptics and naysayers in your midst. Focus on and celebrate your *true* believers—they are going to cheer for you and your book.

Read books that aren't on the best sellers list— after all, if everyone else is reading them, original thought disappears.

Is the publishing siren calling to you? Is it seducing you to tell your story; get your words and wisdom out? To provide answers to someone's problems?

The author is able who believes that he is able.

"The Platform creates the structure for the book," said the blind author as he picked up his pen and was able to see.

*Books fall open,
I fall in—one of my
favorite things.*

When authors love what
they write; when they love
their books, they never have
to work again. What they
do is a sense of joy.

Fill your pages with the
wisdom of your experience
and the
stirrings of your soul.

33

To become an Author
requires blood, sweat
and tears. And for some,
*a little vino, a cup of java
or peach iced tea!*

Smart authors become
savvy positioners.
They do it with **Clarity,
Confidence, Competence**
and **Commitment.**

Words are awesome.
They entertain.
They reveal mysteries.
They solve problems.
They heal. They unite.
They connect.
They create community.

Know the difference between dreams and goals. Goals have plans. Dreams don't.

Ninety-nine percent of authors' first efforts are trashed. It's the *tweaking*, the *rewrites*, the *ahas* along the writing journey that create the book. It's why it's called a "draft."

There is little that is new, new. What is new is the new twist, the new version, the new way to say it and the new way to use it.

To be creative, you must lose the fear of ridicule, being wrong, being different, being vulnerable, sometimes, just being *you*.

Stop thinking about it. Start writing about it.

To the author's surprise and delight, books breed more books.

The joy of being an author: saying with your words what brings the "aha" to the reader.

What separates boring writing from writing that dances? Emotion, as in the lack of it. "Blah" versus "juicy" descriptions. Just telling versus showing loses the reader.

The author's and writer's creed: Butt in the chair. Get to work. Discipline.

*Creativity is getting others
to think you made it up.*

Speed writing with
no plan or topic in mind.
A random word or phrase
can take away the glue
and get you back on
your writing track.

**I love books more than
sharks love blood.**

When your words take
you over; when you wake
in the morning and your
book becomes alive;
you are in the zone.
Own it; breathe it; live it.
What will birth is often
a glorious creation.
And it's yours.

If plan A doesn't work,
the alphabet has 25 more
letters; if you are in Kabardian
(Russia), you've got another 57
to choose from. Japan has 204
characters, which isn't an
alphabet but a great character
may just be what your writing
is seeking. Keep brainstorming.

Beginning and dumping.
Starting again.
It's what we authors do.

*When your intuition tells
you your writing, your scene,
your story, your example,
your fill in the blank
isn't working, it's not.
Stop the bleeding and
get out a blank piece of
paper and let your fingers
take another path.*

Writing is like vomiting ... just let the words and ideas burst up and out. Rinse them off with your rewrites, then edit. You'll feel better in the morning.

A one and a two and a chapter begins to take shape. *A one and a two and a* book unfolds ... **one step at a time.**

Editing and rewriting as you write will slow or stop you. You lose your rhythm. Get it down. *Rewrites are called the next draft.*

41

Learning to write well is a cycle. Most writers suck in the beginning. As they write more, they suck less. As they suck less, they write more. As they write more, they write better. As they write better, they write more. As they write more, they write faster.

Inspiration ... Joy ... and Your Muse:

Morning and Afternoon Delight

Inspiration is elusive. What is the magic cosmic goose for you may be the total turn-off for another. What brings joy and laughter to you may transpire a fellow writer into a spiraling downer.

The key is to find what works for you. Then go to it, embrace it, magnify it, fill your *Writersphere* with its sensations—the sounds, odors, visuals, tastes and touch of the things that bring you calm; that inspire you; that open your creative juices; that allow you to enter into a world that is yours, and yours alone. Bliss and joy.

It could be a marathon of silly movies; a garden of spectacular colors blooming; the surrounding aroma of coffee; the nose of a red wine; a walk on the beach; the pounding of the surf or the flow of a waterfall; the joy of hearing little kids laughing; the deep dive into a favorite book; cooking up a storm;

45

puttering in a shop; the wonder of sunrises
and sunsets; the solitude of a gentle rainfall;
the serenity of a breaking dawn; the
immersion in a lecture … anything that
welcomes the creativity and focus gods.

**It's your *juice* … stuff, environment,
sights, smells, sounds, flavors, happenings,
sensations—the juice that sparks your
ideas and ahas. For the fiction writer,
overhearing a patch of a conversation
seating in a movie theater may seed an
amazing dialogue between characters that
you couldn't get your imagination around;
for the nonfiction business author, it could
be observing and hearing a kaleidoscope
of thunder and lightning as it dances
across the sky that unravels the string of
descriptive metaphors you've been on the
hunt for.**

Your juice is often your *Muse*.
It's critical to know where your creative
juices come from; to know what your
sources are that jumpstart you for any
project that needs your full focus. In today's
multi-media, multi-stimulus, multi-choice
world, it's easy to get off track—the "squirrel
factor." Wham ... in a nano-second, your
attention can be distracted, your body
and mind pulled in an entirely different
direction—it's as if something, sometimes
someone, is clicking a remote control in
your head—pulling you every which way
but in the direction you thought, or wanted,
to go in.

We authors are our own type of warrior
and a Warrior Author needs, must, know
what the driver behind his or her energy
is and feed it—the *Juice*. When it's nourished,
amazing things are accomplished.
Completion of the book. The article.
A book launch planned and executed.

47

Joint ventures with others to spread your message. Marketing plans put in place. The next book started. Etc., etc.

A little joy, a little inspiration, and yes, a little *Juice* will go a long way.

May your Muse be with you!

Always write when you
are inspired. How does
7 am every morning sound?

Waiting for inspiration
will be your downfall.
You might as well wait for
your winning number for
the lottery to be called.
Dive into something with
your words, anything.
Even gibberish.
See what
bubbles up.

The La-Z-Boy chair
was designed for the writer
waiting to be inspired.
It's comfy and cushy.
Don't sit in it.
Inspiration won't come,
sleep will.

Inspiration comes from
off the wall, the seat of the
pants, the push, the school
of hard knocks, from life.
It doesn't come from being
in your comfort zone.

Inspiration is like an unexpected welcome guest. When it drops in, you are thrilled to see it. The question is: what are you going to do until it shows up again?

Stuck? Need a wacky idea to get the creative juices going? Read the tabloid headlines ... weird things seed great ideas.

Authors who wait for their inspiration to show up would be better off finding another date.

51

Books get inspired
when someone or
something stabs you in
the back and instead of
bleeding, you write and
tell the world about it.

The Muse.
The friend to all authors.
It can be animal, vegetable,
mineral. It can be visual,
auditory, sensing.
Identify and welcome
it as your partner.

Knowing *what*—and
sometimes *who*—your
Muse is will kick start
your writing when invited in.
Writing ideas come from
diddling, doodling, boredom,
goofiness, daydreaming,
showering, strolling, TV,
reading, other books ...
ideas flow in all the time.
What you do with
them is what
makes you a writer.

Need help? Don't forget the librarian—she's a master at deep diving into research fields that *Google* has never thought of!

Don't wait for inspiration as you gaze into your belly button. Go after it as if you were famished.

Writers are like sponges. The more we read the genres we write in, the better we get. Read profusely within the genre you want to excel in—it's amazing how the mirror factor begins to come into play.

Whoever you are writing for,
hang out with them so you
know how they think, feel and
act. Otherwise your dialogue
and scenes will be the pits.

Stuck on finding the right
word? There are over
250,000 distinct words
in English alone.
Keep tweaking,
you'll find the right one.

Most people say that they want
to write a book someday ...
the question is: *should they?*

Pure author joy ... when you know that your chapter is *The End* ... and then your mind and fingers start the *Next*.

Writing is like running a race ... you sweat until you cross the finish line.

Dullness is as dullness does. Snap, crackle and pop your words.

You don't want to hang
out with boring people.
Your writing and you will
take on their personality.

Authoring and Writing
are the paths that can lead to
anywhere and **everywhere**.

Even the most
prolific authors
toss a lot of what
they write away.

**There is nothing simple about
writing. It's hard work.**

Writing is not magic...
it can be magical.
Authors. Writers.
Changing the world
one word at a time.

Craftsmanship:
embracing the pursuit
of mastery until your
last writing breath.

Writing Savvy:
The New, New Mantra

Snappy
Sassy
Salty

Ernest Hemingway was the

featured speaker at a seminar. He was hounded by many critics who claimed his books were nothing more than short/mini book reports that he published as books. Why? Simply this: he excelled in using short sentences, short words, short phrases and short paragraphs. His Pulitzer Prize novel, *The Old Man in the Sea*, was created entirely of short sentences, declarative phrases and short paragraphs. The reader didn't need a PhD or a dictionary at his elbow to figure out what they meant.

One pain-in-the-tush critic verbalized that he thought Hemingway was best suited for writing books for children. Period. He said at the seminar to him,

Since you consider yourself the master of short declarative sentences, come up with a story, three sentences, six words, that will move people's hearts.

At the end of the seminar, the same pain-in-the-tush critic stood up and said indignantly, "Well Mr. Hemingway, what is it?"

Imagine Hemingway in his hunting mode persona barking out, "Just a moment, I am still speaking."

When he completed his remarks, he turned and said to the critic, "Here is your story …"

For Sale. Baby Shoes. Never Used.

Wow! A beginning. A middle. An end. Complete in six words. No dictionary needed. Hemingway also said,

Write drunk. Edit sober.

In other words … let it all hang out, dump your thoughts and ideas out … then focus.

That, Dear Author, is a master at work with his words. Something you want to stretch yourself to be with your words. Don't get caught up in what I call "paragraph perpetuity." Keep your words, your phrases, your sentences simple. Your readers will applaud.

Yes, you may be brilliant, have an expansive vocabulary, even a PhD in cross-word puzzles lingo and write long, detailed, tell it all chapters. That's a huge bravo from me to know so much and want to share it all in all your brilliance and glory. But, your reader may not think so.

Let's just say it … sometimes it's a pure joy to have something written that is simply simple, succinct and says all that is needed to be said in a short sentence with "easy" words.

Personally, I vote for the latter.

Stop using "puffy words" in your writing—they clutter it and your voice. Short is better than long.

Don't put off writing the book you really want to write. You may not get the chance.

The book you write is like a mirror—look in it and **discover your heart and soul.**

Reread your favorite book
when you were 10.
What did you love?
What pulled you in?
Carry that magic to
your own writing.

Imagine your reader is sitting
at your table. The story you are
sharing is so compelling that
he can't get up, even to pee.
Now write it.

Are your words merely fillers
... or do they fill the reader,
wanting more?

If it's possible to delete a word,
sentence, paragraph, section,
(gulp), chapter,
without changing the flow
of your writing, *delete it*.

Bypass jargon and
big words when everyday
English can suffice.

If there are sections
in your writing that
are ho-hum,
hit the delete button.
If it's ho-hum to you,
imagine how your reader
may react.

Writing and creating a book
is like cooking.
All you do is glare at a
blank computer screen until
your eyeballs are fried.

Creating and writing a book is
like making a favorite dish.
You know that the main ingredient
is its words. It's all the *spices of
stories, characters, situations,
solutions,* and ideas added that
get the taste buds salivating.

Some authors write the
words. Some authors let the
words write themselves.
The Muse is in play.

Be goofy. Be silly.
Be outrageous.
Awesome and creative ideas
can be the outcome.

For my part, I know that
the sight, the sound, the
smell of water enhances
my creativity.

Savvy authors keep a 'slush'
folder of discarded ideas and
sayings—within may be the
gem you've been looking for.
Your toss-away could become
the Keeper in the next book.

Don't edit when you write,
just write. Let it flow.
Writing and becoming
an author is work.
There is no substitute
in the author's journey.

The fiction writer's best friend
is the palette of emotions:
your reader must *see, hear, taste,
touch* or *feel* through your
words the unfolding story.

Great fiction writers start their
openings with a "hot" start.
Think action verbs
and get the story rolling.

**If you want to get good
at writing; write lots.
If you don't, you won't.**

Savvy writers study the movies.
Get a movie script and dissect it.
Compare it to the book.
Watch the movie.
You will learn how to create a
visual delight with fewer words.
(Tip: get free movie scripts at:
www.Imsdb.com
and *www.SimplyScripts.com*.)

Writers should start on their
books *before* they are ready.
Otherwise, they can spend their
time getting ready in perpetuity.

If you want to be a great writer—read everything you can. Don't expect to become a page-turning author until you get what creates a page turner.

Writers are world-class voyeurs—sometimes in their heads; sometimes on the street.

All who engage in *sex* and *writing* have a lot in common; most start as amateurs—it's only with *practice and experience* that *true expertise* is developed.

72

The difference between a "hot" write and a so-so one: the five senses. When you write with see, hear, taste, touch and feel in your words and descriptions, your words become alive. The reader sees, hears, tastes, touches and feels with you. A fan is born.

When the writing bug hits, embrace it. Don't let anyone or anything in your space. *It's your time.*

Start "hot" in your writing. *Action verbs* start the reader's reading engine and it's off to the races.

There's writing power in one word sentences and one sentence paragraphs. *Use them.*

Planning your writing is not writing. It is planning. *When you create and dive into your words, that is writing.*

74

Write what you know about.
Write what your inquiring mind
wants to learn about.
Write what drops in your lap.
Just write.

Writers don't just dabble.
They write. They tweak.
They rewrite.

Smart writers start with their
heart ... then finish with their
experiences and head.

Political correctness in writing
is boring. Don't write what you
think people want to hear.
Write what you have to say.
In your heart. In your gut.

In writing, use *common words*
to say *uncommon things*
and ideas. Your reader
will thank you.

If the reader needs a cross-word
dictionary to figure out
what you've written,
you are using the wrong words.

Savvy writers leave out all the boring parts.

Write fast. Edit slow. And more than once.

Noodle your words. Finding the right one becomes a moment to salivate over.

Don't use words in your writing
that your reader needs a PhD
or a dictionary close at hand to
figure out what you mean.

Fiction writers have the
nectar gift from the
writing gods. Their
imagination and fingers
know no boundaries.

*Don't write someone else's walk;
walk your own; then write
about it.*

Fiction authors let their characters show them the way. The words they want will follow.

Ruthless editing is the writer's best friend.

Memoirs are a dime a dozen. If your story is unique and different, write it for the world. Otherwise, create copies for your family and friends.

Writing and masturbation
have a lot in common:
both are *frustrating* and
dissatisfying if you don't
finish what you started.

Those who write poetry have
fun—they get to ignore all the
grammar cops and rules.

The most amazing
writing "aha's"
come in the middle of the night
or after a short catnap.

When the author wakes
with first thoughts of his book,
he is in book zone. Cancel
everything else and just write.

Writing is the last frontier: there
are no limits, no boundaries.
Just sheer imagination.

Words and sentences that
don't move your story or
chapter forward are wasted—
delete them.

Don't write the
"fish are in the pond."
Write how the sun glistens
on their spotted backs;
how the setting sun creates
shadows darkening their
brilliant tangerine and salmon
colors; how the scales shimmer
as they effortlessly glide through
the lily pads; how they dash
between the algae and the pellets,
filling their mouths until the
next offering is dropped into the
water. When you do, you've
shown the reader a world not a
word or non-descript phrase.

Writing is like having a mistress: it takes your time, your energy and your money and when you are deep into it, it's ecstasy—you forget about the time, energy and money.

Write "juicy"—your readers will smack their lips with each morsel served before their eyes and mind.

**Sometimes a great
sentence contains
just a single word.**

Page turner creator for authors:
the end of each chapter is
written to make your reader
immediately start on the next.

When the writing bug hits,
writers no longer have to write
… they must write.

Paragraphs aren't meant to
run on in perpetuity.
Think of them as a
morsel to chew on.
Keep them short
for reader ease.

Everything that flows with
your words should be simple
and understandable,
but not simpler.

Failure is NOT an Obstacle:

It's Your Stepping Stone

Sometimes it's not easy being
an author and writer ... there's rejection—
sometimes in a cascading abundance;
sometimes you feel that everything
attempted is a massive flop; sometimes
you think you should be committed for
spending the time and money in creating
your books; sometimes you think there's
no freakin' way you can sell any; and
sometimes you just think ...

But then, a nudge comes into play.
You love your topic. The cover makes you
happy. You remember the unbelievable
sense of pride when you held that first
book in your hand, that first article that is
accepted and has a check tied to it to boot.
A kind word, email, or note comes your way
that you've made a difference, solved a
problem or just provided a new fan with a
terrific story.

To be an author ... to be a writer ... what a journey. Highs and lows. Hopes and fears. Tears and joy. And a journey that requires perseverance. Webster's defines perseverance as *continued effort to do or achieve something despite difficulties, failure, or opposition.*

Isn't that what authors and writers face—sometimes on a daily basis? Are you thrilled with your book sales? Your article production? Would you like to increase them? Sales don't come from luck ... they come from marketing work. And perseverance.

Writing is like an iceberg—5 to 10 percent is the writing; the other 90 to 95 percent is below the surface ... everything that you do to kick start sales, your marketing, and your on-going plan. The continuation of your Book and Author Platforms. Everything.

For sure, this vocation isn't for sissies.
Successful authors and writers have more
rejections than Hogan's got goats. Successful
ones have climbed the wall of dismal sales
more times than they care to count.
Successful authors and writers have received
more negative reviews than their walls have
room to post them on. Successful authors
and writers have had days, sometimes
weeks, months, even years when they have
wondered, "What was I thinking ..."

Yes, we authors and writers don't have it
"easy" as so many believe. It's hard work ...
what separates the successful author and
writer from the non-successful ones?
One word: perseverance.

No author *plans to fail*;
what they do is *fail to plan*.

Mistakes and failures happen.
They become your window to
new ideas and **opportunities**.

All authors bomb at some time.
Get over it. Start again.
Fireworks are in your midst.

Failure in a writing or book attempt is not your enemy. Your enemy is not picking up the pen, turning your computer on and keep writing.

If you don't know where you are going, you've chosen to go nowhere. Any road will do.

When the *Lord of the Rings* books were published … J R R Tolkien became an overnight sensation at the age of 62 with critics who both raved and damned the books.

Authors don't fail ... they fail when they don't learn the lessons that mistakes and previous failures reveal.

Don't be a book polluter. Write what you are aching to say; then tuck it away for a month. Does it now beckon to be allowed out?

Authors' blood type ... All Positive

Every writer and author
struggles. Don't compare yours
to someone else. Every writer
and author experiences
success—the completion of a
paragraph can be celebrated
with a Happy Dance!

Don't get discouraged by
the success of others.
The path you make is *yours*
and *yours alone.*

*Do it, giving up
isn't your option.*

Authors are envied by many—
they want you to rock and do
well. Just not better than them.

Don't fear the critic who
attacks you ... fear the fakes
who surround you.

Keep going ... each step
may get harder ... but don't
ever stop! When you
reach the summit,
the results are spectacular!

It's the rare writer who gets their
piece picked up the first time.
It's the rare author who hits a
homerun every time.

So you failed with your proposal.
Your idea. Maybe you are
ahead of your time, it happens.
Maybe you pitched to the
wrong person, it happens.
Maybe it's not the right fit for
you, it happens. *Start again.*
Tweak or let another
idea birth, it will happen.

The only way you will *succeed*
is to *desire* it more than you
fear rejection or failure.

Failure can be your strongest ally in your progression as a writer. *You go forth wiser, learning from mistakes.*

Total failure happens when you stop trying.

Failure doesn't last forever. Take a bath and wash it off.

Failure is dual-edged: it sinks
those who give up; it inspires
those who dream and plan.

Interesting: failure and success
paths start the same ... they
have a beginning. It's the twists,
turns and detours that you
navigate that determine the
outcome.

Failure is not liking yourself.
Not liking what you write.
Not liking how you write it.
How's that working for you?

Stop living your fears ...
live your dreams. If you believe
your book will be successful,
it's the first step.

**So you were rejected.
What's next? Next is.**

Failure always brings deep
disappointment. You are lost as
an author if you don't try again.

When you give up,
you are guaranteed to fail.

Failure is not a disgrace.
It happens. Get ready for
the next opportunity—it just
might be the giant leap
that makes you the star.

Don't put your energy into
washing walls, hoping a window
will appear. If the book you
are working on isn't working,
put it aside. Start another.

One failure isn't a final failure.

*If you sidestep all failure,
the odds are you avoid
success as well.*

Failure is the master teacher,
not your mortician.

Dr. Seuss was 54 when he wrote *The Cat in the Hat*. What's age got to do with success ... or failure?

Authors and writers can't please everyone ... it's a path to failure.

Why hang out with failure when success is a viable option?

**Wake up.
Kick ass.
Repeat.
Don't you love it?**

If you haven't failed,
you haven't tried!

Success is a 7-Letter Word

It's Elusive, Seductive and Exciting

PUBLISH!

George Gershwin's classic lyrics, "I've got rhythm, I've got music ... who could ask for anything more?" is the perfect element to begin your authoring quest with. Your book has to have rhythm to be successful. Your writing has to have rhythm to be successful. You have to have rhythm to bring it all together. Rhythm connects you to your passion, your heart and your vision. Everything has rhythm to it—the way you live, talk, walk, work, love, eat and play. In *Author YOU: Creating and Building Your Author and Book Platforms*, I shared:

> One of the biggest mistakes authors consistently make is their drive to rush to publish. Rushing without knowing what their flow is really about ... they just know they have a book in them. Slow down. Breathe a

bit. Listen to your rhythm—does it resemble the *Flight of the Bumble Bee, A Hard Day's Night,* or something along the lines of *I've Got Rhythm, Bolero, I Left My Heart in San Francisco* or Louis Armstrong's *What a Wonderful World?*

Is it memorable? Does it have legs? *Rhythm* has flow—everything is connected … you can feel it, you can hear it, and you experience it. Beginner dancers think a lot; when you know the steps, you dance, you instinctively move into and with it. The Art of Authoring and Publishing is no different.

Rhythm has spontaneity to it, usually mixed with a creative flow. For books, rhythm has a synching that occurs between the author and reader. The author starts the lead, the reader follows, trusting the author to take him on a journey that offers pleasure, entertainment or a life-enhancing venture.

Sometimes authors and writers lose their rhythm. John Grisham connected with the reader in his early books. *A Time to Kill, The Firm* and *The Pelican Brief* drew the reader in quickly, opening the door to things unimaginable or unbelievable … the reader was grabbed. Grisham had rhythm with the flow of his form of story-telling. He fell into a routine with his ongoing books that used the law as a backdrop. A dozen plus books later, he hit a rut.

Rhythm is what we are about as authors and writers. And it's the awareness of it that will propel you toward your success. Understanding how to tap into it and how to use it will bring you squarely in front of the mirror: what your book is about; what your writing is about. It is your rhythm— its look, feel and content—it's the song you hear.

Success … it is the author and writer siren that calls out … *come to me, come to me.*

Feeling resistance?
Your new mantra is:
Just Get Over It!

When you know who your audience is; who you are writing for; you pass the first hurdle toward author success.

When you create the *Vision* for you as the author; support it with your *Passion*; *Commit* to it with your time, energy and money—the People will come.

What's *Commitment* got to do with your authoring success? In one word ... *everything!*

Savvy authors have a *Book Game Plan*—they know who they are writing for; what they are writing; where they write best; why they are the one to write it; and how best they write. Then they add in who they need to assist them in making it available; what benefits they bring to the reader; when, where, what and how marketing will be done; and why they are creating the book. The final factor is time and money. How much money is needed to support the book and how much time will be needed to create and support it.

The more you niche yourself as
an author and your book, the
bigger your audience and fan
base will become.

       So you bombed.
Try again. Tweak the next try.
    Make it a better bomb.
Try again. You will succeed.

Avoid the RTP Syndrome.
When you *Rush to Publish,*
you rush to mistakes and chaos.
Guaranteed.

*Authors begin to become successful
the moment they decide to be.*

All goals must have deadlines.
Otherwise they are
only *wishes* or *dreams*.

When it comes to designing
your book, some people are just
the wrong fit. Remove them
from your project and your team.
If you don't, your book will be a
mess. You will be miserable.

Smart authors don't meddle.
The author with moxie selects
good people to do what he
wants done with his book and
is confident enough to get out
of their way while they do it.

Authors should create an ARC
at least three months prior to
publication ... it starts the
buzz, gathers endorsements.

*The more you niche your
expertise, the bigger your
market becomes. You are the
"go to" person. The expert.*

The only difference between a successful writer and one that is a failure: one didn't quit.

If I'm going to be a successful author, it's up to me, starting now.

Persistence and **perseverance**. The two words that separate writing and author failure from success.

An author is a craftsmith.
Words are the tools.
Success is choosing the
right tools for the job.

The big gulp for the author:
taking the leap and saying
with your words: *listen to me,
I have something to say.*

Successful authors are like
televangelists. They believe
in what they write. They are
blatant about promoting it.
They will sell to any and all.

117

The thrill of Book Hill:
the signing of your first book
for your first buyer as others
gather around, waiting for
you to sign theirs.

*Author success factor: you get
paid and use the money to
pay for living expenses.*

Author moxie consists not
so much in knowing what to
do as to what to do next.

Author Delight ...
completing your book and
publishing it to the chagrin
of all the naysayers who said
you couldn't or wouldn't.

Author Ecstasy ...
the arrival of the first copy
of the book. The feel of it;
the smell of it; the vision of it;
the sound of the turning pages;
even the taste of it. *Priceless.*

Marketing Moxie:
The Difference Between Success and Failure

Wouldn't this thing called writing and authoring be so much easier if you could just write and be left alone? If I were to survey a room filled with 1,000 authors and ask how many enjoy marketing and pitching their books when they are published, the odds are that less than 10 percent would enthusiastically say, "Yes indeed, it's what I love to do." Eighty percent would probably want to throw something at me to boot.

Yet, that is exactly what you have to do.

1. You either learn to market yourself. Or …
2. You hire someone to do your marketing for you.

Both will take time. Both will cost you money. The DIY method is mostly time. The Hire It Out method still involves your time and it requires your money.

123

Don't expect an outsider, yes marketing professional, to know all the intricacies of your book—you have to guide them with key concepts, phrases, techniques, strategies— you name it. They will (or should) have venues to dive into that spread the word about you and your book. It's not just the know-hows of marketing; it's the contacts that come into play. Marketing (and publicity) pros should have plenty of them.

Since the great majority of authors are on the side of the fence where they would rather not do it themselves … along with not paying someone to do it for them … my advice is simple and blunt: *get over it.*

Marketing books, and self, is huge work. The results can be staggering when you know your core message and connect it with the ideal reader. Book sales result. Reprints happen. Requests for your appearance at an event come forth. Media is generated. Speaking fees and sponsorships are created.

Not everything will work. Don't toss aside a strategy if it doesn't hit the first time—maybe the timing was off; maybe the wrong people were on your team; maybe you didn't have your 15 second spot-on pitch of what exactly your book is about; what it will do for the reader; and for that matter, exactly who your reader is.

It doesn't happen overnight ... it's one book at a time.

The author's first job
is to write a great book.
The second one is to market it.
There is no third.

Authors who think a publisher
is going to market their books
are in la-la land. Today's author
must learn to and be a master
book marketer. No exceptions.

Stop stabbing yourself in your author back! You cannot afford to kiss-off one more day with Internet book marketing denial. The cyber gods have made it so easy for you to be so outstanding.

Authors: don't treat your books with benign neglect and ignore ongoing marketing. It's the kiss of death decree.

Social media for marketing is not about broadcasting … it's about engaging your followers and fans.

The more you niche who you are writing for, the BIGGER your market becomes.

Marketing and book publishing are *so* Hollywood and more like a house of cards ... few ever do what they promise. You need to be part of a team.

Book marketing is often about hope ... you instill it with a "what if" or "how to" for your reader.

Book success is not about
depth and belly button gazing.
It's about marketing to what
the reader wants or needs
an answer to.

It is all about marketing;
that's where the real craft
comes in. The best books do
not necessarily become the
biggest ones. And vice versa.

Think *Disney* when it comes
to your book marketing. It feeds
and conspires with downright
obsession—you want your
book to be a must have.

When book sales start to come in, *you've hit the marketing sweet spot.*

Create a contest for your book fans to offer up your next book tag line. They know what appeals and hooks them.

Are you just making *noise* with your book marketing or are you creating a symphony?

*Is your marketing as boring
as watching grass grow or
is it a magnificent sunrise?*

If you choose to not market
your book, **you have chosen
to not support it.**

Consider choices for telling
the world about your book.
Then choose one or
some ... but choose.

Eyes wide open—know what you are getting into when you start down the marketing path. It's a commitment and rarely short term.

Your readers are listening in all forms of social media. Find the right one and you will shine.

When you "talk" in social media, your readers and the search engines listen. Are you seeking other ideas for marketing ... or, *are you just inhaling your own exhaust?*

Author Book Marketing is about sharing and telling people about what you care about, what you are passionate about.

When the author talks about their book, it's called *marketing*. People will listen.

Book Marketing is about connecting … finding those who want to hear your story, need your insights, or just want a good read.

Your audience is clickable.
They are hanging out on the Internet.
They may be at a Meetup group
around the corner or a coffee shop.
They could be glued to a specific
social media platform.
They could belong to an association.
They could be *anywhere*
and *everywhere*.

Book marketing today is like
going to the cereal aisle at a
grocery store—all six shelves
of it—and consuming a 60
foot row, packed with every
imaginable type of cereal.
Your aisle is centered on the
Internet. *Go shopping.*

Who knows best, but YOU, the author ... of who your book's market is? *Where do they work? Play? Hangout?* The Internet becomes your magic carpet to transport you and your words ... *Go!*

If it weren't for Edison, we would all be marketing our books by candlelight.

Look in the mirror. No one but the author knows the depths of what a book is about and can do. *You are the voice of marketing.*

135

Don't wait. Yes, there's a *better marketing strategy* and tool out there. But if you wait to discover it, your window may close. Get started. The tools will appear.

Marketing plans are a dime a dozen. Planning is everything and worth far more than a dollar.

It's humbling to say it's impossible or can't be done and watch someone else do it flawlessly.

The benefits of book marketing
are missed by most because
it looks like work.

The Internet for the
Author is the town square
for book marketing today.

After Thoughts ...
The Gift

As I put the final touches on *Snappy, Sassy, Salty*, I was also working with one of my author clients on his fiction book—a creative piece that clearly lands in the "horror" genre. Definitely not my cup of tea for reading pleasure, but I was amazed at how I could morph into his voice; get his mood and attitude; and come up with some gory details all by myself. He was amazed himself and we both laughed about what he called my "odd bent" to the storyline.

I don't have the gift that fiction authors have, in fact, I'm in awe and envy of it— the ability to come up with the most off-the-wall ideas, plots of intrigue/betrayal/ seduction/fantasy that take the reader on a truly delicious reading adventure. What I do have is the gift to "get" where they are and enhance the journey as we work together.

My writing gift is to write nonfiction—
to discover the pain and deep dive into
solutions to relieve and resolve and present
them in a way that my reader gets and
can use.

We all have our gifts—whether it's the
gift to write poetry that amuses and delights
or pulls at the heart strings; the gift to
create warm, wacky, inspiring, romantic,
suspenseful, or futuristic stories that unravel
a magic carpet inviting the reader to "come
to another world …"; the gift to identify
pain and resolve it via an action plan created;
the gift to explain and educate in the massive
"how-to" categories in a language that anyone
seeking can understand; the gift to connect
words to the world of kids; and …

The gifts we authors and writers have
really know no boundaries. Each carries
the most fabulous power. Here's to us!
Here's to you!

Judith

Meet Dr. Judith Briles

Judith Briles is the author of 31 books—18 published with New York houses until she created Mile High Press in 2000. Based in Colorado, she's published in 16 countries and with over a 1,000,000 copies sold of her work. ***Author YOU: Creating and Building Your Author and Book Platforms*** was a #1 bestseller on Amazon. ***Show Me About Book Publishing*** co-written with book marketing guru John Kremer and master book publicist Rick Frishman. ***Snappy, Sassy, Salty: Wise Words for Authors and Writers*** is her latest.

Judith is the Founder and Chief Visionary Officer of Author U (university), a membership group of hundreds of authors and small publishers and the Colorado Authors Hall of Fame.

She is a partner in *MastersofBookMarketing.com* with Dan Poynter and Brian Jud.

She is a past president of the Colorado Authors League, has chaired numerous publishing conferences and is a frequent speaker at writer and publishing conferences.

Judith knows publishing and she gets the challenges that authors go through in creating and publishing their books. Known as The Book Shepherd to many, she's personally guided hundreds of publishing clients throughout the United States, Canada and Australia. Each fall, she hosts *Judith Briles Unplugged*, a two-day exclusive "happening" for authors who want to be successful with practical authoring and publishing guidance.

Her websites are:

www.TheBookShepherd.com

www.AuthorU.org